P9-BYW-257

To:

From:

Designed by
Kerren Barbas

Illustrations copyright © 2002
Steve Haskamp

Text copyright © 2002
Peter Pauper Press, Inc.
202 Mamaroneck Avenue
White Plains, NY 10601
All rights reserved
ISBN 978-0-88088-170-8
Printed in China

21 20

Visit us at www.peterpauper.com

Reach
for the
Stars

You gain strength, courage and confidence by every experience in which you really stop to look fear in the face.

ELEANOR ROOSEVELT

Life is either
a daring adventure or nothing.
To keep our faces toward change
and behave like free spirits
in the presence of fate is
strength undefeatable.

HELEN KELLER

Our greatest glory
is not in never falling but in
rising every time we fall.

CONFUCIUS

Go confidently in the
direction of your dreams!
Live the life you've imagined.
As you simplify your life,
the laws of the universe
will be simpler; solitude
will not be solitude,
poverty will not be poverty,
nor weakness weakness.

HENRY DAVID THOREAU

When you get into
a tight place and
everything goes
against you, till it
seems as though you
could not hang on
a minute longer,
never give up then,
for that is just the
place and time
that the tide will turn.

HARRIET BEECHER STOWE

Now, go ahead,
reach for the stars!

Success is how high
you bounce when you
hit bottom.

GEORGE PATTON

People often say that this or
that person has not yet
found himself. But the self is
not something that one finds.
It is something that one creates.

THOMAS SZASZ

The images you
send out about
yourself into the
world determine
how other people
see you.

SANAYA ROMAN

I have learned
that success is to be
measured not so much
by the position that
one has reached in life
as by the obstacles
which he has
overcome while
trying to succeed.

BOOKER T. WASHINGTON

We cannot escape fear.
We can only transform it
into a companion that
accompanies us on all our
exciting adventures. . . .
Take a risk a day—one
small or bold stroke that
will make you feel great
once you have done it.

SUSAN JEFFERS

It's so important to believe in yourself. Believe that you can do it, under any circumstances. Because if you believe you can, then you really will.

WALLY "FAMOUS" AMOS

Expect the best;
convert problems
into opportunities; be
dissatisfied with the status
quo; focus on where you
want to go, instead of where
you're coming from; and
most importantly, decide
to be happy, knowing
it's an attitude, a habit
gained from daily
practice, and not a
result or payoff.

DENIS WAITLEY

It is only the first step
that is difficult.

MARIE DE VICHY-CHAMROND,
MARQUISE DU DEFFAND

You can have anything you want
if you want it desperately enough.
You must want it with an
inner exuberance that erupts
through the skin and joins the
energy that created the world.

SHEILA GRAHAM

I don't want to get
to the end of my life and
find that I lived just the length
of it. I want to have lived
the width of it as well.

DIANE ACKERMAN

Every moment of your life
is infinitely creative and the universe
is endlessly bountiful. Just put forth
a clear enough request, and everything
your heart desires must come to you.

SHAKTI GAWAIN

When your every
thought and your
every action is directed
to your ultimate life
goals, you become
unstoppable and assured
of great success
and happiness.

ROBIN S. SHARMA

Believe in yourself!
Have faith in your
abilities! Without
a humble but reasonable
confidence in your
own powers you cannot
be successful or happy.

NORMAN VINCENT PEALE

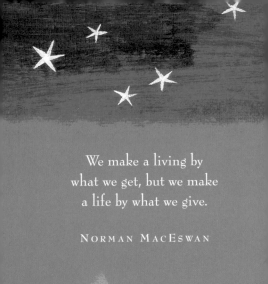

We make a living by
what we get, but we make
a life by what we give.

NORMAN MACESWAN

Reach high, for stars lie
hidden in your soul.
Dream deep, for every
dream precedes the goal.

PAMELA VAULL STARR

Power comes from living
in the present moment,
where you can take action
and create the future.

SANAYA ROMAN

When will you realize
that "today" IS the "tomorrow"
you hoped for "yesterday"?

KEN KEYES, JR.

Real joy comes not
from ease or riches or from
the praise of men, but from
doing something worthwhile.

W. T. GRENFELL

There are people
looking for exactly what
you have to offer, and you
are being brought together
on the checkerboard of life.

LOUISE L. HAY

You have a right
and a responsibility
to lay claim
to what touches
you and effects
change for the future.

Jodie Foster

To look out at you
gives me enormous hope.
You look so competent,
so strong, so young,
so committed, so ready
to take on the future,
difficult times and all.

COLIN POWELL

God grant me
the serenity to
accept the things
I cannot change,
courage to change
the things I can,
and the wisdom
to know the
difference.

REINHOLD NIEBUHR

Life is a grindstone,
and whether it grinds
you down or polishes
you up is for you and
you alone to decide.

CAVETT ROBERT

You have powers
you never dreamed of.
You can do things you never
thought you could do.
There are no limitations
in what you can do except
the limitations of your
own mind.

DARWIN P. KINGSLEY

Boldly walk
into tomorrow with a
purpose and a vision
for a better world.

HENRY LEO BOLDUC

The most beautiful
thing we can experience
is the mysterious.

ALBERT EINSTEIN

Good character is a prerequisite to happiness. It entails empathy, courage, generosity, work, honesty, discipline, and balance. It is not easily achieved. It is not a lesson which can be learned from books. It requires practice.

JEANE J. KIRKPATRICK

The foolish man seeks
happiness in the distance;
The wise grows it
under his feet.

JAMES OPPENHEIM

Happiness is a habit—
cultivate it.

ELBERT HUBBARD

Every person has
a purpose and a reason
for being on earth.

SANAYA ROMAN

Don't worry about
what the world wants from you,
worry about what makes you
come more alive. Because what
the world really needs are people
who are more alive.

LAWRENCE LESHAN

We must not only give
what we have, we must
give what we are.

DÉSIRÉ-JOSEPH MERCIER

I believe in myself.
I believe in my vision, my life,
my talent, my art. More
than anyone. No one can
take that away from me.

SABRINA WARD HARRISON

The future has
several names.
For the weak,
it is the impossible.
For the faint-hearted,
it is the unknown.
For the thoughtful
and valiant,
it is the ideal.

VICTOR HUGO

Aim at a high mark
and you'll hit it.
No, not the first time,
nor the second time.
Maybe not the third.
But keep on aiming
and keep on shooting
for only practice will
make you perfect.

ANNIE OAKLEY

Lots of people want to ride with you in the limo, but what you want is someone who will take the bus with you when the limo breaks down.

OPRAH WINFREY

The place to improve
the world is first in one's own
heart and head and hands.

ROBERT M. PIRSIG

It occurred to me when
I was 13 and wearing gloves
and Mary Janes and going
to dancing school, that no
one should have to dance
backward all their lives.

JILL RUCKELSHAUS

Everyone has talent.
What is rare is the courage
to follow the talent to the dark
place where it leads.

ERICA JONG

That's what being young
is all about. You have the courage
and the daring to think that you can
make a difference. You're not prone
to measure your energies in time.

RUBY DEE

Standing in the
middle of the road
is very dangerous.
You get knocked
down by the traffic
from both sides.

Margaret Thatcher

Light tomorrow
with today.

Elizabeth Barrett Browning

True life is lived
when tiny
changes occur.

LEO TOLSTOY

Everyone has
in him something
precious that is
in no one else.

MARTIN BUBER

The reason why
most people
miss opportunity
when it comes along
is because
it comes dressed
in work clothes.

BRIAN TRACY

Accomplishments
have no color.

Leontyne Price

I like dreams
of the future better
than the history
of the past.

Thomas Jefferson,
in a letter to John Adams

True miracles are created
by men when they use the
courage and intelligence
that God gave them.

JEAN ANOUILH

The dictionary
is the only place
where success
comes before work.

ARTHUR BRISBANE,
QUOTED BY BENNETT CERF

Cherish
your friends
and family
as if your life
depended on it.
Because it does.

Ann Richards

While we are
influenced by
circumstances,
we, too,
can have an
influence.

JONAS SALK

Respect
yourself.
Listen to what
you *really want*
and follow
your instincts—
they are
usually right.

JERILYN ROSS

All of us
have to remember
where we came from
and what it was like then
if we are to understand
where we are heading
and how to get there.

COLIN POWELL

Change is the law of life.
Those who look only
to the past or present are
certain to miss the future.

JOHN F. KENNEDY

Live your heart's
passion. Do whatever
it is that excites your
inner light and passion.
Live exuberantly with
purpose and excitement.
TRULY MAKE
YOUR DAILY LIFE
AN ADVENTURE.

HENRY LEO BOLDUC

An entrepreneur
is someone willing
to go out on a limb,
having it cut off
behind her, and
discovering she had
wings all the time.

LEIGH THOMAS

No one can really pull
you up very high—you lose
your grip on the rope.
But on your own two feet
you can climb
mountains.

LOUIS BRANDEIS

Life is like a wild tiger.
You can either lie down
and let it lay its paw on
your head—or sit on its
back and ride it.

SUSAN HAYWARD

Life is a personal mission.
You have a calling that
exists only for you and that
only you can fulfill.

NAOMI STEPHAN, PH.D.

If I have the belief
that I can do it, I shall surely
acquire the capacity to do it, even
if I do not have it at the beginning.

MAHATMA GANDHI

It is not because things are
difficult that we do not dare;
it is because we do not dare
that they are difficult.

SENECA

Nothing can dim
the light which shines
from within.

MAYA ANGELOU

To be who you are
and become what you
are capable of is the
only goal worth living.

ALVIN AILEY

A life filled
with celebration is
a rich one indeed.

DONALD O. CLIFTON
AND PAULA NELSON

The best way
to predict your future
is to create it.

STEPHEN R. COVEY